YODHA-II

ILLUSTRATED MILITARY HISTORY OF INDIA

The Crown (1858) to The Kargil War (1999)

For my father, Ashok Kalyan
Who always charted his own path
And insisted my every work
Set a new benchmark

YODHA-II

ILLUSTRATED MILITARY HISTORY OF INDIA

The Crown (1858) to The Kargil War (1999)

SHIV KUNAL VERMA

CHETW

BUILDING

Yodha-II: Illustrated Military History of India—The Crown (1858) to The Kargil War (1999)
by Shiv Kunal Verma

978-93-92210-99-0
First edition 2024

Published by:
JGS Enterprises Pvt Ltd
Imprint: The Browser | Fauji Days

Publisher's Address:
SCO 14-15, FF, Sector 8-C, Chandigarh 160 009
service@thebrowser.org

Photographs & Text: Shiv Kunal Verma

Printed in India

Layout and Cover Design © 2024 by beagles
99beagles.com

thebrowser.org
Publishers & Booksellers

faujidays.com
Oral History and Military Publishing

CONTENTS

Maritime Jaguars ▸

◄ INS *Godavari*

Shiv Kunal Verma

Introduction

The uprising of 1857 was not the first mutiny or rebellion that took place on Indian soil. The Vellore Mutiny of 1803 is the most well-known instance, but the Madras and Bengal Sepoy Armies had had a fair share of disturbances. The British response in the aftermath of the uprising was so ruthless, with 'rebels' being tied to cannons and blown to bits, that even the rest of India that had not got involved trembled with fear. The East India Company, who today would be classified as 'organised looters', were replaced by the Crown. The message was not lost on the remaining Princely States, for few dared to take on the British Raj, which left no stone unturned in its quest to create the majesty of governance.

This was also the time of the birth of the new Indian Army. Just as British India had adopted Akbar's administrative methods, they took many concepts that Maharaja Ranjit Singh had innovated while raising his army. The idea of 'martial races' was advocated and adopted, and just about every pillar of India's diverse culture was subverted especially the education system. The railways and their development across the subcontinent gave the British Raj the

mobility to tighten their grip on the subcontinent further.

The concept of 'frontiers' now took on a new meaning. The coastal regions, by their very nature, were well-defined, but the northern and eastern regions were ambiguous. British expansion went into the next phase as Bhutan, Sikkim, and Tibet were in the Himalayas, and Manipur, Nagaland,

and Mizoram in the Naga Patkai saw various expeditions. Indian troops were also used to fight in various other parts of the globe, as was the case with the Boxer Rebellion in China and even the Maori Uprising in New Zealand.

What happened then is spelt out in this volume in fair detail, but suffice it to say that by the time World War II (WWII) ended, the Indian Armed Forces had been honed into one of the finest fighting forces anywhere in the world. However, Subhash Chandra Bose's Azad Hind Army and the Ratings Mutiny in the Royal Indian Navy had clearly given the British the signal that they could not necessarily play Indians against each other, especially within the armed forces. President Roosevelt's diktat to Winston Churchill before the Americans entered WWII also meant the old world order had to change soon.

But then, the British had not been the rulers of an empire 'where the sun never set' without being masters of subterfuge and devious divide-and-rule policies. Since the end of World War I (WWI), they had been planning to split India into two parts, and in the mid-1930s, Churchill had recruited a disillusioned Mohammad Ali Jinnah into his two-nation ploy, which was then bought by the Muslim League and the Congress. Ironically, the strength of the British had been to push India's frontiers as far to the west, north and east as possible. The first thing 'free' India's and Pakistan's leaders did was to let boundaries be created that ran across the very heart of the subcontinent. The carnage that resulted because of the Partition ensured that the two sides would remain at each other's throats!

The subcontinent was divided for good. To add to the problem, first Sinkiang and then Tibet came under Chairman Mao's People's Republic of China (PRC) after they had pushed the Kuomintang government out of the mainland into Formosa (Taiwan) in 1949. All of a sudden, the Indians had a new hitherto non-existent neighbour across a nearly 4,000 km long border. Sardar Vallabhai Patel, the Indian Home Minister, wrote to Prime Minister Nehru 17 days before his death that the PRC was by its very nature expansionist and that they were unlikely to honour the treaties the Tibetans had with British India.

The biggest saving grace for the Indians was that they had managed to force the British to set up the Indian Military Academy (IMA), which

had started to train an Indian officer cadre that would supplement the few King's Commissioned Indian Officers (KCIOs). Generals Thimayya, Thorat and 'Bogey' Sen had commanded battalions during WWII and had been battle-inoculated, as had the IMA graduates like Sam Manekshaw and others. Almost all these officers were fast-tracked into the higher ranks. Pakistan, too, benefitted, as almost all their senior officers post-Partition had been commissioned from the IMA.

There is enough evidence to suggest that British officers masterminded the blueprint for the invasion of Jammu & Kashmir in October 1947. A most telling moment was when Bogey Sen, the commander of the 161 Brigade that was to fly into Kashmir, met Mahatma Gandhi, who told him that he (Sen) must use every means at his disposal to fight the raiders to protect the lives and properties of the people. Fighting in the most difficult situations, the Indian Army of Independent India would set the bar for itself.

Hardly tested in Hyderabad and Goa, the Indian Army's clash with the People's Liberation Army (PLA) in 1962 came as a rude shock. India's defence preparedness was at its nadir, and the country paid a huge price even though in North-East Frontier Agency (NEFA, now Arunachal), the Chinese pulled back to their earlier positions almost immediately. For all practical purposes, the clash with Pakistan three years later was a continuation of the same conflict, as India's western neighbour tried to instigate a similar defeat. The Indian Air Force (IAF), not used in an offensive role in 1962, was brought into action even as the Pakistanis launched Operation Grand Slam, and with India's political leadership under Prime Minister Lal Bahadur Shastri going for the kill in Lahore and Sialkot, the dynamics of warfare in the subcontinent changed altogether.

In 1971, a belligerent Pakistan Army supported by Razakars had turned on its own people and the genocide that was unleashed in East Pakistan was horrific. With 10 million refugees pouring into India, it was but a matter of time before the Indians responded. In two weeks the Indian Armed forces had, through a force of arms, created a new country and bagged 93,000 POWs. For the Pakistani Military junta, often referred to as an 'army with a country' rather than the other way around, it was a telling blow. However, the raison d'etre of Pakistan has been an anti-India stand, so the conflict continues in one form or the other, be it the Siachen Glacier or the Kargil conflagration in 1999. This volume draws to a close with the turn of the century, but Fortress India continues to face many challenges. To meet them, we must understand the past.

Combing Lok Tak Lake

RAJPUT Colours on Parade

Reorganisation

Post-1857 CE

Post-1857, the failure of the uprising, combined with the brutality with which the British responded, left the subcontinent stunned. The Government of India Act of 1858 was an act of the British Parliament that transferred the government and territories of the East India Company (EIC) to the British Crown. With Queen Victoria's formal proclamation on 1 November 1858, the EIC's rule over

▲ The Crown's colours stored at the Indian Military Academy

▲ British ships on the river Hooghly; British and Native Sikh Officers 1858

British territories in India came to an end, and it was passed directly to the British government. The Indian Army was overhauled, trade was brought back to normal, and the reforms planned for the Indian educational system were fast-tracked by the British.

In the previous volume, we saw Indian history as it unfolded from mythological times to ancient times, and with each turn of the page, we saw empires and dynasties come and go. The medieval period saw not just the arrival of invaders from the north but

▲ One of the biggest casualties of the 'Mutiny of 1857' was the Indian education system. A school in Calcutta (above) and a girls' school in Jaipur, Rajasthan, are representative of the countless ***gurukuls***, ***madrassas***, and monasteries that educated Indians across the sucontinent. To change the thinking of 'the natives', the British went about systematically destroying the old order. In 1813, the renewal of the EIC's charter carried a duty to educate and assist previously excluded Christian missionaries in educating the population, in addition to the Company's corporate activities. English education meant modern education; A portrait of a Koli chieftain of Dahewan (right)

also the arrival of a religious ideology in the form of Islam. After the fall of the Vijaynagar Empire to the combined forces of the Deccan Sultans, the entire dynamics of the subcontinent changed dramatically.

The arrival of the Portuguese on the west coast of India in 1498 more or less coincided with the arrival of the Mughals under Babur. Though the Dutch followed suit soon after, the Portuguese, for almost a century, zealously guarded the sea routes and, in the process, fortified parts of the west coast. The arrival of the British and then the French expanded their global rivalry to India as well, and soon, they were locked in a tussle for the control of the lucrative Carnatic belt. As they established themselves, both sides had to deal with multiple challenges. Solutions to overcome these invariably depended on their relations with the 'natives', be they nawabs, sepoys in their armies, or their vast bevy of servants who they had in their employ. Until around 1820 (which coincided with the end of the Third Maratha War), EIC officers and their families viewed India and Indians as some sort of oriental mavericks who were different but at par with them. Perhaps the ease with which the formidable Mughal Empire collapsed and then numerically superior forces lost to the British time and again made the EIC officials look at the Indians as being an inferior race.

By 1857, this attitude had given way to contempt and arrogance, and the complete lack of sensitivity to Hindu and Muslim sentiment had led to the uprising. The equation between the Indians and the Europeans not only led to the conquest of the

The Princely state of Baroda, having sided with the British in 1857, was the first state to adopt the new educational policies ▼

subcontinent but also played a key role in consolidating colonial rule. The EIC, on its part, neither had the means nor the knowledge to operate without the tacit support of Indian rulers, especially in the eighteenth century, when the British were establishing themselves. Indian rulers who would strike alliances with the British, having calculated how it would give them a strategic edge over their rivals, would then find themselves in a bind as they became more and more dependent on the colonials for their own survival.

Post 1857, the British, having decided to stay on, needed to create two groups of Indians who would help them keep the rest of the country in chains.

The Presidency Armies were henceforth part and parcel of the British Indian Army, and all Native Infantry and other arms changed their nomenclature, though they retained the Battle Honours that had been bestowed on them as a part of the EIC forces. The Jonathan Peel Commission, which had the task of reorganising the Indian Army in the post-1857

The Umbeyla campaign was undertaken between Oct–Dec 1863 against Muslim tribesmen in Sittana and focused on the village of Malka. The tribesmen had harboured Indian mutineers in 1857 and were still resisting British rule over a decade later. The Yusafzai Field Force under General Sir Neville Chamberlain advanced up the Umbeyla Pass against strong opposition ▼

scenario, identified social groups and regions from which 'loyal' soldiers could be recruited. The emphasis was that the native army should be composed of different nationalities and castes and mixed judiciously through each regiment. Caste, religion, and ethnicity or race became more crucial while enlisting a soldier. Greater Punjab now became a major catchment area for the Bengal Army, and the Bombay and Madras Armies began to be looked upon as being definitely inferior to the Northerners. Sikhs, Pathans, Baluchis, and some selected Muslim communities, besides Gurkhas and Dogras, began to be known as the 'martial races'.

The British had been toying with the idea of replacing the age-old Indian educational system even before 1857. They had successfully sold the narrative that Indian society was in a moribund state rooted in age-old traditions and evil practices like *sati,* and it was up to the 'white man' to pull them out of the clutches of wicked rulers who were thriving after the

collapse of the Mughal Empire. They chose to ignore the fact that India was already a complex and thriving society even before the Portuguese, Dutch, British, and French arrived. On the contrary, colonialism was a parasitical system that needed to also exploit the human resources of the host country. The obvious and most effective method was to then revamp the entire educational model.

▲ A group of Indian Army Officers and Non-Commissioned Officers, all holders of the Indian Order of Merit seated and standing under an exterior archway

Until 1835, when the British politician Thomas Babington Macaulay presented his 'Minute on Indian Education', which sought to establish the need for Indian 'natives' to receive an English education, the Indian educational system was centred around *gurukuls* and *madrassas*, where the medium of education for Hindus was Sanskrit, and for the Muslims, it was Arabic and Persian, along with the various vernacular languages that were in use in different parts of the country. Macaulay suggested the EIC should not spend any resources on Indian institutions, and among other things, he argued that just a small number of Indians should receive government education in order to get jobs in government administration and other positions that would help serve British interests. These suggestions had been on the back burner, but after the 1857 uprising, these would become the 'Holy Bible' for subsequent committees to proceed on.

The ruthlessness with which the British had come down on the rebel sepoys and their earlier victories over the Marathas and others had left a major mark on the psyche of the rulers of all Indian princely states. Though on the face of it, the British had, after the 1857 uprising, made concessions towards Indian 'sensibilities', their grip on Indian affairs had further tightened.

Baroda, one of the biggest princely states, was looked at by the British as a 'loyal state'. In 1857, when Khande Rao Gaekwad received the news that a number of Koli Talukdars and Bhils led by two brothers, Nathaji Patel and Yamaji Patel, were planning to revolt against him and the British, he stationed his cavalry at Chandap to quash the rebellion. However, the Baroda cavalry was defeated and thrown out by Kolis of Chandap with tremendous losses. The Kolis, their numbers upto around 2,000, occupied the Taranga hills and continued their rebellion for a few months. By the end of October 1857, the combined forces of the British, Idar State, and Baroda attacked the Kolis and Bhils and sacked the Chandap village.

Adopting guerrilla tactics, the Koli chieftains and Bhil soldiers then attacked Gaekwadi villages near Ahmedabad, and they continued their resistance around the Sabarmati River till the end of 1858. The Kolis would subsequently pay a huge price for their resistance to the British. They were not only defeated in battle and punished for having dared to resist, but, in the aftermath of the uprising, the Kolis were disarmed and also marginalised by the rest of society as outlaws and forced to practise agriculture. The message to all communities was loud and clear – you were either subservient to the British or simply marginalised.

Troopers from Skinners Horse ▼

The Himalayan kingdom of Bhutan, protected by Vaishravana, the semi-wrathful Buddhist god who is the leader of the North, and Four Directional Guardians ▸

Bhutan 1864–65 CE

The Bhutan War, or the Duar War, was fought between British India and Bhutan in 1864–1865. The British government had sent a peace mission to the Himalayan kingdom in early 1864 after the conclusion of a civil war there. The *dzongpon* of Punakha, who had emerged victorious, had broken ties with the Bhutanese central government and had set up a rival *druk desi*, which was the office of the spiritual head, while the legitimate *druk desi* sought the protection of the *ponlop* (governor) of Paro. The British mission dealt alternately with the rival *ponlop* of Paro and the *ponlop* of Tongsa (the latter acting on behalf of the *druk desi*), but the Bhutan government rejected the peace treaty.

In response to perceived slights against British envoys involved in the ongoing negotiations, John Laird Mair Lawrence, the governor-general of India, ordered a declaration of war on Bhutan in November of 1864 despite the fact that Bhutan had no regular army, and the forces that existed were composed of dzong guards armed with matchlocks, bows and arrows, swords, knives, and catapults.

Four columns of British, Indian, and Gurkha troops, known as the Duar Field Force, marched north into the Bhutanese foothills and captured the four forts at Dewangiri, Sidli, Buxa, and Daling by January 1865 relatively easily. At this point, the majority view was that the pacification of Bhutan had been completed, and there were even orders issued for the demobilisation of the Daur Field Force when attacks by the local Bhutanese forces began across the entire line of captured forts and British-Indian positions.

Tented campsite in foreground with mounted and dismounted soldiers near the tower on the edge of a mountain ▼

▲ Despite impressive forts, other than dzong guards,Bhutan did not have a standing army. The seat of central government was at Thimphu, the site of a thirteenth-century dzong, in the spring, summer, and fall. The winter capital was at Punakha, a dzong established northeast of Thimphu. The kingdom was divided into three regions (east, central, and west), each with an appointed ***penlop*** (governor) holding a seat in a major dzong. Districts were headed by dzongpens, who had their headquarters in lesser dzongs

▲ The Bala Pass and the fort of Dalimkote that were stormed by the British forces on 15 February 1865

Whilst the majority of the attacks, such as those on the troops stationed at Buxa, were repulsed, the attacks against the fort of Dewangiri at Deothang had the defenders in serious trouble. Bhutanese forces managed

◄ Ashley Eden forced by the Bhutanese to sign a treaty in 1864. The British, especially sensitive to any diplomatic slights, declared war against the Himalayan kingdom

to both cut off the water supply and communication routes to the fort, placing the British troops at the mercy of their own dwindling ammunition supplies. Before dawn, on the morning of 5 February, the defenders of Dewangiri staged a breakout, but the attempted withdrawal became confused and led to the loss of the majority of the force's baggage, guns, and even some of the wounded.

Once news of these disasters reached Calcutta, strong reinforcements in the shape of two brigades, led by the Victoria Cross (VC) holder Brigadier-General Tombs, were sent to take back the initiative. The renewed force managed to retake Dewangiri by April 1865, with Bakhat Singh Rai of the 44th (Sylhet) Regiment of Bengal Native (Light) Infantry being awarded the Indian Order of Merit for leading the charge to storm the Bhutanese stockade. When the British recaptured the Dewangiri fort, they dismantled it.

The main Duar War lasted only five months. Despite some battlefield victories by the Bhutanese, the clash resulted in Bhutan's defeat. The war would drag on in smaller engagements for many more months until the guns lost in the retreat from Dewangiri were finally returned, ending hostilities. Under the terms of the Treaty of Sinchula, signed on 11 November 1865, Bhutan ceded sovereign territories in the Assam Duars and Bengal Duars as well as the 83 square kilometre territory of Dewangiri in southeastern Bhutan in return for an annual subsidy of 50 000 rupees.

▲ The Tiger's Nest Monastery

Lushai Hills

1871 CE

British expansion and consolidation over Assam and the surrounding Naga Patkai hill areas continued apace with the Lushai expeditions that would continue over the next two decades. The Lushai Hills (known as Mizoram today)—stretched southwards from Silchar towards Chittagong and Cox's Bazaar, both important ports on the Bay of Bengal—was the southern part of

▲ British officers trying to get Mizo chiefs to help free hostages

Assam that was under the control of the East India Company since 1824.

The first recorded Kuki raid happened in 1826, and after that many people lost their heads. Punitive raids into the Lushai Hills by the British Army had invariably floundered because of the hostile terrain and excessive rainfall. In 1850, the magistrate of Sylhet reported a series of massacres by 'Kookis' in what was alleged to be British territory, in which 150 persons had been killed. Matters came to a head in 1871 when there were multiple raids, among which, in one case, British subjects had been captured. The hostages included a six-year-old girl called Mary

Mary Winchester would also become the rallying call for Christian missionaries ►

Winchester. Yet another punitive expedition then set out to rescue the child and convince the hill tribes of the region that they had nothing to gain and everything to lose by placing themselves in a hostile position against the British government.

The British decided that two columns would advance after the rains, the first under General Brownlow, advancing from Chittagong, and the second under Mr Edgar, the deputy commissioner of Cachar, with General Bourchier advancing from Cachar. In addition to these two columns, a contingent of Meiteis accompanied by Colonel James Nuttall, the Political Agent of Manipur, made its presence felt across the southern border to co-operate with General Bourchier's portion of the expedition. Both the columns met considerable resistance but succeeded in destroying the chief village of the offending raiders. Mary Winchester was rescued after a year in captivity.

Sacrificing a Mithun to seal a 'blood treaty' with a Lushai chief ▾

The Great Game

The Great Game, or *Bolshaya Igra,* was the dramatic enmity between the British and Russian Empires in Central Asia. The rivalry started in the nineteenth century and continued through to 1907 as Britain sought to control much of Central Asia to buffer its empire in India. The Great Game's scholarly usage can be traced back to a lecture

◄ The Remu Glacier in the Upper Shyok Valley as recorded by the military expedition to Yarkhand and Kashgar under Sir Douglas Forsyth. The expedition would chart the route to the Russian frontier and also the Oxus sources on the Pamir. A published account of the journey would catapult London into hysteria over what would be known as the Great Game as the British and the Russians jostled to establish their supremacy over the roof of the world. It was a compelling drama, and the public, not just in Britain, India, and Russia, lapped it up. The Great Game severely impacted almost all countries of Central Asia

delivered by Professor HWC Davis to the British Academy on 10 November 1926 entitled *The Great Game in Asia (1800–1844)*.

The term signified two historical developments. The first was the series of alleged activities of secret British and Russian agents across Central Asia. Such agents were invariably tasked with the collection of information carrying some sort of political or military value. Almost without exception, these agents, referred to as 'assets' in Intelligence circles, were also tasked to lay the foundations of a strong political influence over the native population. However, most of the information gathered, at least during that period, was handled carefully and never leaked into the public domain. This initial jockeying to establish their spheres of influence by both British and Russian agents is looked at as the first phase of the Great Game by most scholars.

The second and more popular phase was the overt actions of the British and Russians to garner as much influence as possible. With the rivalry between the two powers no longer being a secret, the developments focused on the question

King Amanullah Khan receiving military aircraft from the Soviet Union [c.1924–c.1925]. In 1924, the Soviet Union again gave military aid to Afghanistan, including small arms and aircraft, and conducted training in Tashkent for cadre officers from the Afghan Army The aeroplanes received from the Soviet Union, complete with pilots and mechanics, became the foundation of the Afghan Air Force. For the next decade, Soviet pilots performed the bulk of the flying of Afghan aircraft, many of which were Polikarpov R-1s, a Soviet copy of the de Havilland DH9A. Most Afghan aircraft were destroyed in the civil war that began in December 1928

of India's defence against any invasion from the West. It is quite possible that the first Anglo-Afghan War was its direct outcome. Most of the debates that took place in later years often led to mass hysteria in London, with numerous articles catching the public imagination and raising questions on whether to stay on the current frontier or advance into Central Asia, on whether to try to form buffer states or to forgo dealings with Central Asia and rely solely on British power, and whether to oppose Russia or to work toward an agreement with her. The British Lord Ellenborough triggered off this phase of the Great Game on 12 January 1830 with a decree establishing a new trade route from India to Bukhara, using Turkey, Persia, and Afghanistan as buffers against Russia to prevent it from controlling any ports on the Persian Gulf. Meanwhile, Russia wanted to establish a neutral zone in Afghanistan, allowing them access to crucial trade routes. It was later established that while Russians did want a buffer state, they had no plans to enter Jammu & Kashmir or British India. The British Raj, on the other hand, became so obsessed with the issue that they spent a huge amount of time and effort to secure the frontiers of British India. This resulted in a series of unsuccessful wars for the British in an attempt to control Afghanistan, Bukhara, and Turkey. Ironically, the fallout of this was in Russia taking control of several Khanates, including Bukhara. Although Britain's attempts to conquer Afghanistan ended in humiliation, the independent nation did become a buffer between Russia and India. It finally ended with the Anglo-Russian Convention of 1907, which divided Persia into a Russian-controlled northern zone, a nominally independent central zone, and a British-controlled southern zone.

The Great Game impacted the geopolitical scenario, which not only coloured events at that time but continued to do so even two centuries later. 'The Tournament of Shadows' was dominated by Western writing, while on the Russian side, there was the Polish-Lithuanian orientalist and explorer, the enigmatic Captain Yan Vitkevich. Many Indians played an active part, of which the three Pundits, Mohan Lal Kashmiri, Nain Singh Rawat, and Sarat Chandra Das, all explorers and scholars in their own right, particularly stand out.

Moorcroft, disguised as a horse trader, makes his way into Central Asia ▾

An 1875 portrait of Queen Victoria painted by the Austrian portraitist Henrich von Angeli ▸

Delhi Grand Durbar
1877 CE

Two decades after the 1857 uprising, the British could take stock of the situation and feel they had not only survived the 'hiccup' of the 'mutiny' but had actually emerged a lot stronger, wherein they had virtual, if not absolute control of the Indian subcontinent. The message to all princely states and independent rulers was loud and clear. Maharajas tried their best to be even more British than the

British, competing with each other to arrange tiger hunts for British royalty while the Raj was steadily expanding its footprint across the globe. Meanwhile, Indian troops of the revamped army were even serving overseas as the Empire continued to be the most powerful entity on the planet, with the sun never setting on the 'British Empire'.

Philip Mason calls it the 'Majesty of Governance' in his book, *The Men Who Ruled India*. The dust having settled down, the British felt the need to hold a visual demonstration of British imperial rule, and accordingly, the Delhi Durbar was convened. On 1 January 1877, in Delhi's Coronation Park, Queen Victoria took on a new title: Empress of India, or *Qaisar-i Hind*. The main event of the *jalsah-i-qaisari*, or the Delhi Durbar as it is commonly called in English, was Victoria's proclamation. The subjugation of India and its people was complete. About 70,000 spectators, including 15,000 British and Indian soldiers, attended the ceremony. It turned out to be a show of military prowess for the colony. Over the

◀ The 'Majesty of Governance' in full display at the *jalsah-i-qaisari* that was held at Delhi

▲ The Maharaja of Baroda's procession

Popular writers like Rudyard Kipling would play their part in romanticising the British Raj ▶

course of a 14-day celebration and feasting, 63 Indian princes and other dignitaries joined the Crown's Viceroy of India, Robert Bulwer-Lytton, and the various British governors. For the first time in Indian history, Indian aristocracy had united around the shared objective of honouring the British monarchy.

Queen Victoria, however, was not present during the ceremony. Her proclamation speech as the new ruler of India was read aloud to the assembly of Indian and British citizens in both Urdu and English by Lord Lytton. A number of tall promises that included liberty and dignity for all were made in the speech but were discarded soon thereafter. The British, who were masters of the game, gifted all

On 1 January 1877, in Delhi's Coronation Park, Queen Victoria took on a new title: Empress of India, or Qaiser-i Hind.

◄ A native officer from the 13 Bengal Lancers while stationed in Malta

Indian rulers of princely states continued to lead a lavish lifestyle ▼

the attending princes gold souvenirs, thereby asserting their paramountcy over all of India. In the end, the Durbar achieved its aim of reminding Indians of their subordination to the British Empire and a declaration of imperial power and control over their country.

Second Afghan War 1878–79 CE

The conflict between the British and Russians, as the Great Game intensified, had its flashpoint in Afghanistan. Following the Congress of Berlin in June 1878 that aimed at curtailing the growing Russian influence in the Balkans and the Mediterranean after the defeat of the Ottomans in the Russo-Turkish War of 1877–78, there was a temporary easing of tensions in Europe. However, the Russians then shifted their focus to Central Asia, adding fuel to an already simmering fire. Russia dispatched an unannounced diplomatic mission to Kabul that

◂ The Ninth Queen's Royal Lancers during Sir Frederick Robert's march to Kandahar, 1879

same summer. The Amir of Afghanistan, Sher Ali, made an unsuccessful attempt to keep the British out, but when the Russian envoys arrived in Kabul on 22 July 1878, the British insisted that Sher Ali accept their mission as well. Not only did the Amir again decline, but he also threatened to thwart any mission entry into Afghanistan if one was sent.

On 21 November 1878, the viceroy, Robert Bulwer-Lytton, decided to call Sher Ali's bluff and issued an order for a diplomatic delegation to go to Kabul. The Second Anglo-Afghan War began after the expedition had to be abandoned when it was not allowed to go beyond the Khyber Pass. The British then mobilised a 40,000-strong force that was divided into three fighting columns that then entered Afghanistan. Sher Ali unsuccessfully tried to personally plead with the Tsar for help and fled to Mazar-e-Sharif, never to return.

The British offensive was swift, and soon, they were controlling a vast area of Afghan territory. Yaqub, the son and heir of Sher Ali, signed the Treaty of Gandamak in May 1879 to stop the British from penetrating further. In accordance with this arrangement, Yaqub gave the British authority over Afghan foreign affairs in exchange for an annual subsidy and guarantees of support in the event of foreign assault. Afghanistan gave Britain control over a few of its frontier areas like Khyber and Michini passes.

The second campaign ended in September 1880 when the British defeated Ayub Khan and invited Abdur Rahman Khan to be the new Amir who ratified the Gandamak treaty. Having created the buffer between the Raj and the Russian Empire, British and Indian soldiers then withdrew from Afghanistan.

the Kabool Gate, Jellalabad. 28 Dec.

Mahomed Ghol,
Duranee,
Jellalabad,
Wm Simpson.

Left Page: (left column, top to bottom)
The 1st Sikhs, coming out of the Kabool Gate, Jellalabad, 20 December 1878; Horse artillery struggling to get past the Khyber Pass

Left Page: (right column, top to bottom)
Picquet of the 4th Goorkhas, Basawul, 12 December 1878; Arrival of Sir Fred Haines, Commander-in-Chief, at Jellalabad, 28 February 1879; A prisoner brought in after the battle of 2 April

Right Page: (top)
An Elephant Battery with 40 Pounders at arrival at Jellelabad; Touted as the 'Revenge for Maiwand' and labelled as 'Victory at Kandhar' the charge of lancers at the edge of a river on 1 September 1880

Right Page: (bottom)
Group of five officials seated in a tent during the negotiations for the Treaty of Peace, at Gandamak in May 1879

Manipur 1891 CE

The kingdom of Manipur owed its freedom from the seven-year-long tyranny of Burmese control in 1826 to the Manipur Levy. By 1835, a British political agent was placed to oversee the working of Raja Gambhir Singh, thereby formally colonising the state. A string of family feuds and palace intrigues followed, and as the kingdom spiralled

The royal procession coming out of the Kangla Fort in Imphal, The fort, though mostly in ruins now, was the center of temporal power for centuries Manipur; The palace revolt came to a head when the Political Officer Frank Grimwood was killed in March 1891

into a decline in the second half of the nineteenth century, the power of the British agent increased manifold, making him the defacto ruler.

Internal disputes between the princes and the tendency on the part of the British to meddle with their affairs created an ugly situation on 24 March 1891, wherein the British troops stormed the palace, killing many innocents, including unarmed women and children. The very next day, a group of British officers went to the castle again, this time without an escort, to talk peace. However, as they were exiting the palace, they were jostled and severely wounded by an angry crowd. Soon after that, they were beheaded by the locals on the orders of a senior military functionary of the state. On 31 March, orders were issued by the British government to put an end to the uprising. Three strong columns were dispatched to attack Manipur from three different directions. While the Manipuris fought hard, the numerical superiority and flexibility enjoyed by the British resulted in the kingdom's fall to the British.

Subsequently, after a hasty trial, senior leaders of the uprising were hanged to death on 13 August 1891. Many others were also given capital punishment and were executed between 25 May and 13 October. Since then, 13 August is observed as the Patriots' Day.

Manipuri artists, over the years, have successfully kept the memory of those who fought in the palace revolt alive ▼

◄ The Kangla Sha is a sacred guardian beast with a lion's body and a two-horned dragon's head

Skilled horsemen and adept at fighting the Burmese, the Manipuri Army was no pushover ▼

The Assam Rifles consisting of troops that were better equipped and drilled, slowly made their way to Imphal; Advancing on three fronts, a British column advancing from Burma

Anti-Clockwise (from top left):

The British column that advanced from Kohima preparing to March on Imphal

The British blowing the Royal symbol of the Manipuris, the Kangla Sha

Bir Tikendrajit was appointed the Senapati of the Manipur Army after the palace revolt

The statue of Major General Paona Brajabashi (1833–1891) at Khongjom

After the British had regained control of Imphal, they made sweeping changes and banished the old guard to the Andamans

The second column from Silchar fighting off an ambush laid by the Manipuris

Maharaj Sheodan Singh of Alwar (1845–74) ▸

The State Forces

By the beginning of the twentieth century, there were more than 550 princely states, of which 58 maintained armed forces to a standard fit for use in the defence of India if needed. These states chose to join the Imperial Service Troops scheme, established in the late 1880s, which made their troops available for service alongside the Indian Army when such service was requested by the British government. The armies of the princely states were bound by many restrictions that were imposed by subsidiary alliances. The British undertook

124th Duchess of Connaught's Own Baluchistan Infantry ▶

▼ 14th Murray's Jat Lancers

▲ 20th Deccan Horse, earlier 1st Lancers Hyderabad Contingent

◀ 11th King Edward's Own Lancers (Probyn's Horse)

to contribute equipment and weapons to the forces units of the states on payment. In return, the princely states were required to bring the pledged troops up to a level of preparation that would enable them to serve alongside regular Indian regiments. Kashmir was the first of the participating states to provide a contingent for active service when two mountain batteries fought in the Hunza Nagar campaign of 1891 and the subsequent Chitral Expedition of 1895. Alwar, Bikaner, Jodhpur, and Malerkotla provided units for service in China during the Boxer Rebellion of 1901.

◂ An officer from the Patiala Lancer–Imperial Service Corps (1901)

An officer and a sowar from the Prince of Wales Bhopal Lancers (1905); Nizam of Hyderabad's cavalry in 1838–40

Group of Indian Army officers outside the Buckingham Palace